D0385930

BOSTON COMMON PRESS
Brookline, Massachusetts

2000

Other titles in the *Cook's Illustrated*
How to Cook Series:

HOW TO
SAUTÉ

An illustrated step-by-step guide to
sautéing chicken, turkey, and veal cutlets;
pork medallions; steaks; fish fillets and
steaks; shrimp; and scallops.

THE COOK'S ILLUSTRATED LIBRARY

Illustrations by John Burgoyne

Boston Common Press
17 Station Street
Brookline, Massachusetts 02445

ISBN 0-936184-39-6
Library of Congress Cataloging-in-Publication Data
The Editors of *Cook's Illustrated*
    How to sauté: An illustrated step-by-step guide to sautéing chicken,
turkey, and veal cutlets; pork medallions; steaks; fish fillets and steaks; shrimp; and
scallops./The Editors of *Cook's Illustrated*
1st ed.

    Includes 48 recipes and 22 illustrations
    ISBN 0-936184-39-6 (hardback): $14.95
    I. Cooking. I. Title
2000

Manufactured in the United States of America

Distributed by Boston Common Press, 17 Station Street, Brookline, MA 02445.

Cover and text design: Amy Klee
Recipe development: Kay Rentschler, Bridget Lancaster, and Julia Collin
Series editor: Jack Bishop

CONTENTS

introduction

I RECENTLY HAD A LIVELY DISCUSSION WITH A FOOD writer who claimed that cooking is about "the spur of hunger and the pleasing of appetite." He was taking exception to cooks who believe, as I do, that cooking is a great deal about process and who insist on taking a methodical, detailed approach to the process of preparing and cooking food. Of course, neither of us is right. Cooking is about many things, including the spur of hunger and the science of cooking. The simple sauté illustrates how these two approaches can work in harmony.

A quick sauté (cooking food in a hot pan with a modicum of fat) is, on the surface, the ideal recipe for the passionate cook who, spurred on by hunger, takes a well-worn pan and a few simple ingredients to please the appetite. Having tasted the results of my early sauté attempts and those of many other home cooks, I know that the promise often exceeds the reality. Butter easily burns in a hot pan, overcrowding results in steaming instead of sautéing, and fussing with the chicken breasts or cutlets disturbs formation of a good crust. Of course, the wrong pan and a fear of high heat can also wreak havoc with this seemingly simple cooking process.

To give home cooks a good foundation to work from, our test kitchen set out to determine the principles of sautéing. Once mastered, these principles can be applied to a wide range of dishes involving chicken, fish, pork, turkey, lamb, and beef, plus literally thousands of quick pan sauces. The dishes can be as simple as sautéed chicken cutlets with a lemon caper sauce, as unusual as sautéed fish fillets with a chipotle orange sauce, or as traditional as steak served with red wine sauce. One can marry the mastery of technique with last-minute improvisation, becoming a scientist and a poet at the same moment.

How to Sauté is the nineteenth book in a series of "how to" titles published by *Cook's Illustrated*, a bimonthly publication about American home cooking. Turn to the beginning of the book for a complete list of titles in our How to Cook Series. To order books, call us at (800) 611-0759 or visit us on line at www.cooksillustrated.com. For a free trial copy of *Cook's*, call (800) 526-8442.

Christopher P. Kimball
Publisher and Editor
Cook's Illustrated

chapter one

SAUTÉ BASICS

T O SAUTÉ IS TO COOK FOOD QUICKLY IN A hot skillet. In general, you need just enough fat to coat the bottom of the pan. If you add enough fat to reach any measurable depth, then you are pan-frying, not sautéing.

Sautéing causes the exterior of meat, poultry, and seafood to brown. Browning adds flavor to foods and promotes the development of a crisp crust, which offers a pleasing textural contrast with the interior of foods. Sautéing is usually reserved for tender, quick-cooking, boneless cuts, such as chicken cutlets or fish fillets.

Besides browning the food, sautéing produces flavorful

browned bits in the pan, which can be used to make a quick sauce once the cooked meat, poultry, or seafood has been set aside.

In some cases, the meat, poultry, or seafood can be coated with bread crumbs and then sautéed. This produces an especially crisp crust. In order to preserve the crunch of the breading, we don't serve breaded cutlets and fillets with a pan sauce.

This book focuses on sautéed main courses suitable for a quick weeknight dinner. Individual chapters explore chicken cutlets; turkey and veal cutlets; pork medallions; steak; fish fillets and steaks; and shrimp and scallops. All of these foods are boneless and require almost no preparation on the part of the cook.

Although it is quick, sautéing is not always simple. Too often, foods don't brown as well you might like. Sometimes the kitchen fills with smoke. At other times, foods stick to the pan.

This chapter covers the basics—from how to handle food before it goes into the skillet to how to make pan sauces. For details on sautéing specific foods, see the appropriate chapter.

▌▌ MAKE SURE THE FOOD IS DRY

Moisture is the enemy of sautéing. Not only does moisture cause hot fat to splatter, but it also prevents browning.

Foods should always be thoroughly dried with paper towels just before they are sautéed. For the same reason, you shouldn't season foods too far in advance. Over time, salt draws moisture to the surface. Try sprinkling foods with seasonings while you wait for the pan to preheat.

◼ FLOUR DELICATE FOODS

We find that some foods with a delicate texture, such as chicken cutlets and flounder fillets, benefit from flouring before cooking. The flour coating promotes browning and ensures that the exterior crust will be crisp. In our testing, we found that sturdier meats, such as steak, should not be floured; they brown well without any coating. Also, shellfish can absorb flour and become gluey, so we don't recommend flouring shrimp or scallops.

◼ CHOOSE THE RIGHT PAN

When sautéing you will need a large pan that can accommodate as much food as possible in one batch. Food that is crowded into a small skillet won't brown as well, especially if all the food is not in direct contact with the pan bottom. Also, crowding food into a small pan causes the temperature to drop precipitously, which negatively affects browning. It is also important to choose a pan with a heavy bottom.

In theory, cast iron would seem to be a good choice for sautéing; in fact, however, it is not recommended because it can react with some acidic pan sauces. Heavy stainless steel pans with an aluminum or copper core, such as those manufactured by All-Clad, or heavy anodized aluminum pans, such as those made by Calphalon, are our favorite choices in the test kitchen. We like these pans because they are heavy and conduct heat evenly across the entire bottom of the pan.

Avoid thin, inexpensive stainless steel or aluminum pans. Food and pan drippings are far more likely to burn, especially at the high temperatures we recommend throughout this book.

We tested nonstick and enamel-coated pans and found them acceptable but not quite up to par. Fat tends to bead up on these slick surfaces and so may not coat foods evenly once they are added to the pan. As a result, foods don't brown as well in nonstick and enamel-coated pans. A bare metal surface yields more intense color and thus more flavor.

▚ PREHEAT UNTIL BLAZING HOT

Too often, home cooks are timid about using high heat on their stove. Yes, you may make a bit of mess on the stovetop, but high heat is the only way to brown four steaks at once. In addition, foods can stick in cool pans, something that never happens in a hot pan.

In each recipe, we recommend heating an empty skillet over high heat for a specific amount of time. Do not skip this step.

USE VEGETABLE OIL

We find that neutral-tasting oils, such as vegetable, peanut, or canola, make the best medium for sautéing. Olive oil can clash with flavorings in the sauce. It is also more likely to burn. Butter adds a delicious flavor to sautéed foods, but the danger of burning is great. Even when blended with some vegetable oil, butter usually burns. Save butter for swirling into the finished pan sauce.

We prefer to add the oil to a hot pan, not a cold one. Add the oil all at once and swirl it over the pan bottom. The oil will shimmer immediately, indicating that the pan is ready for food.

PLEASE DO NOT DISTURB

Despite the origin of the word *sauté*, which means "to jump" in French, it's critical to let the food sit after it hits the pan if it is to form a good crust. Resist the temptation to check it constantly. All that activity cools the food down, getting in the way of browning and making the food more likely to stick to the pan. Lifting the food from the pan too early can also cause the crust to tear.

12

If you like, set a splatter screen—a round mesh screen with a handle—over the skillet to minimize the mess on your stovetop. The screen keeps fat in the pan without causing foods to steam, as they would if covered with a lid.

▚ DEGLAZE THE EMPTY PAN

Once sautéed foods are browned and cooked through, they should be placed on a plate in a warm oven while you use the pan drippings to make a quick sauce. Start by sautéing aromatics (garlic, shallots, onions) in the drippings. Next, deglaze the pan with some liquid (anything from stock to vinegar to bottled clam juice) and scrape with a wooden spoon to loosen the flavorful browned bits. You then simmer the liquid until it reduces to a nice, thick consistency. Other ingredients, such as mustard and herbs, can be added to the sauce.

We like to finish most sauces by swirling in some softened butter. The butter enriches the sauce and gives it more body. Swirl in the butter off heat with a wooden spoon so that the butter does not separate.

In restaurants, pan sauces start with veal, chicken, beef, or fish stock. In a nod to convenience, we call for canned low-sodium chicken broth for the recipes in this book. If you have homemade stock on hand, use it. Stock has more body than canned broth (the former usually contains gelatin from bones) and will improve the texture as well as the flavor of pan sauces.

▣ CHOOSE THE RIGHT SAUCE

Although the technique we use to make pan sauces is pretty much the same throughout the book, the texture and flavor of the sauces vary so as to complement specific sautéed foods. For instance, shrimp requires a thick glaze that can really cling to each piece. Citrus works with seafood but might seem odd with beef, which tastes better with heartier flavors such as red wine, mushrooms, brandy, peppercorns, and cream.

Once you master the basics of sautéing and making a pan sauce, you will be able to create your own recipes almost without effort. Pick up some cutlets, fillets, or steaks on the way home from work and then use pantry staples and whatever else you have on hand to create a pan sauce. The 48 recipes in this book are a starting point; once you've mastered the basic techniques, hundreds of variations will be within your grasp.

▣ USE HOMEMADE CRUMBS

In some recipes, we coat foods with bread crumbs before sautéing. A crisp, breaded cutlet or fillet does not require a pan sauce. A squirt of lemon juice will suffice.

We tested a number of different coatings and found that homemade bread crumbs are superior to store-bought. Homemade crumbs are larger and more irregular in shape and therefore promote a crisper crust. We liked cornmeal but felt that it could not serve as an all-purpose coating, as do bread crumbs. (Fish fillets are an exception; they really benefit from the extra crunch that cornmeal adds.)

To make homemade crumbs, simply grind small cubes of stale bread in a food processor until fine. Choose a bread without seeds or sugar when making homemade crumbs. Of course, you can substitute an equal amount of store-bought crumbs if you like.

As for liquids to dip the food in before coating it with crumbs, we tested egg, milk, and a combination of milk and egg. Lightly beaten egg (thinned with a little water) makes the lightest, crispiest coating. We also found that flouring the cutlets and fillets before dipping them in egg and then bread crumbs helps the food to retain moisture and produces the crispiest coatings.

chapter two

CHICKEN CUTLETS

AUTÉING A BONELESS, SKINLESS CHICKEN BREAST sounds easy. But too often the chicken comes out of the pan only lightly colored and dry. Ideally, a sautéed chicken breast should have a nicely browned exterior and a tender, juicy interior.

We sautéed both floured and unfloured chicken cutlets to determine any differences in taste, texture, and juiciness. We immediately noticed a more dramatic sizzle when the unfloured cutlet hit the pan. While both cutlets sizzled during cooking, the unfloured cutlet "spit" a bit more. The flour seems to provide a barrier between the fat in the pan and the moisture in the cutlet. The floured cutlet also moved

16

about more freely; while neither version stuck to the skillet, the floured cutlet skated easily as we swirled it about.

When cooked, the floured cutlet displayed a consistently brown crust, almost resembling a skin. The uncoated breast was a spotty brown. Both breasts were equally moist, but the floured cutlet had a better mouthfeel, with its contrasting crispy exterior and juicy, tender meat. The floured cutlet, reminiscent of fried chicken, was also more flavorful than its uncoated counterpart. Our advice: Flour those cutlets.

The best cooking medium for chicken cutlets is vegetable oil, which provides excellent browning and won't burn. In a concession to the reigning wisdom about health, we tried sautéing a batch of cutlets in just the sheerest film of fat. The results were disastrous. The fat burned, the outside of the chicken became dry and stringy, and the crust was very disappointing, nearly blackened in some spots and a strange yellowish color in others. For sautéed food to become crisp and uniformly brown, the entire surface must stay in contact with the fat. Chicken has an irregular surface, and any part that is not in contact with the cooking medium—in this case, the oil—will not brown because it is being steamed by the moisture released from the cooking meat. In a 12-inch skillet, two tablespoons of oil is about right. If your skillet is wider, you may need closer to three tablespoons.

Everyone's stove is different, of course, but most home burners are quite weak, so when we say "high," we mean "high." Once the oil shimmers, quickly lay in the chicken cutlets, with the tenderloin-side down, holding onto the tapered end as you lay the cutlet flat.

Maintain the heat to the point at which the fat remains at a fast sizzle but does not quite smoke. If you see more than just a wisp or two of smoke, slide the pan off the burner immediately, turn down the heat, and wait a few seconds before returning the pan to the flame. Be advised that there will be some spattering.

We also tested coating the cutlets with bread crumbs to make an especially crisp exterior and found that breaded cutlets tended to burn faster than regular floured cutlets. We made several modifications to our basic sautéed chicken cutlet recipe to eliminate this problem. First, the cutlets must be pounded to a thickness of a half-inch or less so that the interior won't still be raw when the exterior has browned. Second, the pan doesn't require as much preheating. Last, breaded cutlets should be cooked at a slightly lower temperature than plain floured cutlets.

♛

Master Recipe

Sautéed Chicken Breast Cutlets
serves four

➤ **NOTE:** *Serve the chicken breast cutlets plain or with any of the sauces on pages 20 through 26.*

4	chicken breast cutlets (1½ pounds), trimmed (see figure 1, page 26), tendons removed (see figure 2, page 26), rinsed, and thoroughly dried
	Salt and ground black pepper
¼	cup all-purpose flour
2	tablespoons vegetable oil

⁞⁞ INSTRUCTIONS:

1. Preheat oven to 200 degrees. Place a plate in oven for keeping cooked cutlets warm while making sauce.

2. Sprinkle both sides of cutlets with salt and pepper to taste. Measure flour onto a plate or pie tin. Working with one cutlet at a time, dredge in flour. Make sure tenderloin is tucked beneath and fused to main portion of breast (see figure 3, page 27). Pick up cutlet from tapered end; shake to remove excess flour.

19

3. Heat heavy-bottomed 12-inch skillet over high heat until hot, about 4 minutes. Add oil and heat briefly until it shimmers. Lay cutlets in skillet, tenderloin-side down and tapered ends pointing out (see figure 4, page 27).

4. Adjust heat to medium-high (fat should sizzle but not smoke) and sauté cutlets, not moving them, until browned on one side, about 4 minutes. Turn cutlets with tongs (a fork will pierce meat); cook on other side until meat feels firm when pressed and clotted juices begin to emerge around tenderloin, 3 to 4 minutes. Remove pan from heat and transfer cutlets to warm oven. Continue with one of the sauces that follows.

▪▪ PAN SAUCES:

Lemon-Caper Sauce
enough for 4 servings

1	medium shallot, minced
1	cup canned low-sodium chicken broth
¼	cup lemon juice
2	tablespoons small capers, drained
3	tablespoons unsalted butter, softened

Follow Master Recipe for Sautéed Chicken Breast Cutlets (page 19). Without discarding fat, set skillet over medium

20

heat. Add shallots; sauté until softened, about 30 seconds. Increase heat to high, add broth, and scrape skillet bottom with wooden spatula or spoon to loosen browned bits. Add lemon juice and capers; boil until liquid reduces to about ⅓ cup, 3 to 4 minutes. Add any accumulated chicken juices; reduce sauce again to ⅓ cup. Off heat, swirl in softened butter until it melts and thickens sauce. Spoon sauce over chicken and serve immediately.

Sherry-Cream Sauce with Mushrooms
enough for 4 servings

➤ **NOTE:** *White wine, champagne, port, or Madeira can be substituted for the sherry in this classic chicken sauté; in that case, the mace should be omitted or replaced by a speck of nutmeg.*

2	medium shallots, minced
8	ounces thinly sliced mushrooms
⅓	cup sherry, preferably cream or amontillado
½	cup canned low-sodium chicken broth
1	cup heavy cream
2	tablespoons minced fresh parsley leaves
	Pinch of ground mace
	Salt and ground black or white pepper
1	small lemon wedge

Follow Master Recipe for Sautéed Chicken Breast Cutlets (page 19). Without discarding fat, set skillet over medium heat. Add shallots; sauté until softened, about 30 seconds. Increase heat to high, add mushrooms, sauté until soft and brown, 2 to 3 minutes. Add sherry; boil until sherry completely evaporates, about 1 minute. Add broth and cream; boil, stirring frequently, until sauce reduces to ⅓ cup and is thick enough to lightly coat a spoon, about 5 to 6 minutes. Add any accumulated chicken juices; reduce sauce to previous consistency. Stir in parsley and mace and season to taste with salt, pepper, and drops of lemon juice. Spoon sauce over chicken and serve immediately.

Tomato-Basil Sauce with Capers
enough for 4 servings

2–3	shallots, minced (about ⅓ cup)
3	medium garlic cloves, minced
2	medium-large tomatoes, peeled, cored, seeded, and chopped (about 2 cups)
¼	cup dry white wine or 3 tablespoons dry vermouth
2	tablespoons small capers, drained
2	tablespoons shredded basil leaves or minced parsley leaves
	Salt and ground black pepper

Follow Master Recipe for Sautéed Chicken Breast Cutlets (page 19). Without discarding fat, set skillet over medium heat. Add shallots and sauté until softened, about 30 seconds. Stir in garlic, then tomatoes. Increase heat to high and cook, stirring frequently, until tomatoes have given up most of their juice, forming a lumpy puree, about 2 minutes. Add wine, capers, and any accumulated chicken juices; boil sauce until thick enough to mound slightly in a spoon, about 2 minutes. Stir in herb and season with salt and pepper. Spoon sauce over chicken and serve immediately.

Asian-Style Sweet and Sour Sauce
enough for 4 servings

3	medium garlic cloves, minced
2	teaspoons minced fresh gingerroot
¼	teaspoon hot red pepper flakes
¼	cup dark brown sugar, packed firm
¼	cup distilled white vinegar
2	tablespoons soy sauce
½	teaspoon anchovy paste or Asian fish sauce
4	medium scallions, including the tender green parts, thinly sliced

Place garlic, ginger, and pepper flakes on a cutting board; mince further to pulverize the pepper. Follow Master

Recipe for Sautéed Chicken Breast Cutlets (page 19). Without draining fat, return skillet to medium heat; add garlic mixture and sauté until softened, about 30 seconds. Increase heat to high; add brown sugar, vinegar, soy sauce, anchovy paste, and accumulated chicken juices; boil, stirring to loosen browned bits from pan bottom until mixture thickens to a light syrup, less than 1 minute. Pour sauce over chicken, scatter scallions on top, and serve immediately.

Mustard and Cream Sauce with Endive and Caraway
enough for 4 servings

1	medium head endive, cut diagonally into ¼-inch slices
2	medium shallots, minced
2	tablespoons cider vinegar
1	teaspoon caraway seeds
½	cup canned low-sodium chicken broth
½	cup heavy cream
1	teaspoon Dijon mustard
	Salt and ground black pepper

Follow Master Recipe for Sautéed Chicken Breast Cutlets (page 19). Without draining fat, return skillet to medium heat; add endive and shallots; sauté until softened and lightly browned, 3 to 4 minutes. Add vinegar and bring to boil, scraping up browned bits from bottom of skillet with wooden spoon. Add caraway seeds, broth, and cream; increase heat to medium-high and boil, stirring occasionally, until slightly thickened and reduced to generous ½ cup, about 5 minutes. Stir in mustard and season to taste with salt and pepper. Pour sauce over chicken and serve immediately.

Peach Salsa
enough for 4 servings

2	small peaches or nectarines, cut into small dice
½	large cucumber, peeled, seeded, and cut into small dice (about ⅔ cup)
1	plum tomato, seeded and cut into small dice
2	tablespoons chopped red onion
1	jalapeño chile, stemmed, seeded, and minced
4	teaspoons lime juice
	Salt
1	cup canned low-sodium chicken broth
2	teaspoons lemon juice (or additional lime juice)

1. Mix peaches, cucumber, tomato, onion, chile, and lime juice in medium bowl. (Can cover and refrigerate up to 24 hours.) Before serving, season salsa with ¼ teaspoon salt or to taste; set aside at room temperature and follow Master Recipe for Sautéed Chicken Breast Cutlets (page 19).

2. Pour off any remaining chicken fat, set skillet over high heat; add broth and boil until it reduces to ⅓ cup, scraping up browned bits from pan bottom. Add any accumulated chicken juices and reduce sauce to previous consistency; stir in lemon juice. Pour sauce over chicken. Spoon salsa alongside chicken and serve immediately.

Figure 1.
Lay each cutlet tender-
loin-side down and
smooth the top with your
fingers. Any fat will
slide to the periphery,
where it can be trimmed
with a knife.

Figure 2.
To remove the tough, white
tendon, turn the cutlet ten-
derloin-side up and peel
back the thick half of the
tenderloin so it lies top
down on the work surface.
Use the point of a paring
knife to cut around the tip of
the tendon to expose it, then
scrape the tendon free with
the knife.

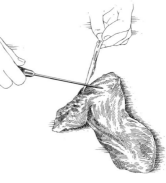

Figure 3.
When flouring, make sure that the tenderloin is tucked beneath
and fused to the main portion of the breast.

Figure 4.
To avoid being splashed with hot fat, lay the cutlets into the pan
thick side first and hang onto the tapered end until the whole
cutlet is in the pan. The tapered ends of the cutlets should be at
the edges of the pan, where the heat is less intense.

27

Master Recipe

Sautéed Breaded Chicken Cutlets

serves four

➤ **NOTE:** *If you can buy thin cutlets (no thicker than ½ inch), skip the pounding step. These thin cutlets can be sliced and served over a bed of greens or served in a sandwich roll. Unlike regular sautéed cutlets, breaded cutlets are delicious at room temperature and can be packed for picnics.*

1	large egg
1	tablespoon water
1	cup bread crumbs, preferably homemade (see page 15)
¼	cup all-purpose flour
4	chicken breast cutlets (1½ pounds), trimmed (see figure 1, page 26), tendons removed (see figure 2, page 26), rinsed, and thoroughly dried
	Salt and ground black pepper
3	tablespoons vegetable oil

▓ **INSTRUCTIONS:**

1. Whisk egg with water in small, flat bowl. Measure bread crumbs and flour onto separate plates or pie tins.

2. Pound cutlets to thickness of ½ inch (see figure 5, page 31). Season cutlets with salt and pepper to taste, then dredge them one at time in flour, knocking off excess. Using tongs, dip each cutlet in egg wash, letting excess drip off (see figure 6, page 32), then place in pan with crumbs. Press crumbs lightly onto cutlets with fingertips to ensure that they adhere to surface of cutlet (see figure 7, page 32). Transfer breaded cutlets to baking rack to dry for 5 minutes (see figure 8, page 33).

3. Heat heavy-bottomed 12-inch skillet over medium-high heat until hot, about 2 minutes. Add oil and heat briefly, just until it shimmers. Lay cutlets in skillet, tenderloin side down and tapered ends pointing out (see figure 4, page 27).

4. Maintain medium-high heat, so fat sizzles but does not smoke, and sauté cutlets until golden brown and crisp on one side, about 3 minutes. Check underside of cutlets once or twice to make sure they're not coloring too quickly. If they look very brown, lower heat slightly. Turn cutlets with tongs (a fork will pierce meat); lower heat to medium and cook on other side until meat feels firm when pressed, about 3 minutes. Serve immediately or transfer cutlets to plate in 200-degree oven to keep warm. Serve warm or at room temperature. (Cutlets may be refrigerated for 1 day. Bring to room temperature before serving.)

▪▪ **VARIATIONS:**

Sautéed Breaded Chicken Cutlets with Lemon and Herbs

Follow Master Recipe (page 28), replacing water in egg mixture with equal amount of lemon juice and adding 1 tablespoon chopped fresh dill, tarragon, oregano, or thyme to bread crumbs.

Sautéed Breaded Chicken Cutlets with Parmesan (Chicken Milanese)

Follow Master Recipe (page 28), reducing bread crumbs to ¾ cup and combining crumbs with ¼ cup grated Parmesan cheese. Serve with lemon wedges.

Sautéed Breaded Chicken Cutlets with Cornmeal Crust

Follow Master Recipe (page 28), reducing bread crumbs to ¼ cup and combining crumbs with ¼ cup yellow cornmeal. For a spicy coating, add cayenne pepper to taste to cornmeal-bread crumb mixture.

Figure 5.

Chicken cutlets that are to be breaded should be ½ inch thick or less. The coating on thicker cutlets will burn before the cutlet cooks through. If you have one, use a heavy-duty meat pounder or smooth-sided mallet. If not, use an empty wine bottle or the flat side of a chef's knife to flatten the chicken. Start by removing excess fat and the tendon. Place the cutlets, tenderloin-side down, on a cutting board. Lay the side of a large chef's knife on the breast and pound with your fist to flatten the cutlet to the desired thickness.

Figure 6.
We bread all chicken, veal, and turkey cutlets as well as fish fillets
according to this process. To avoid breading your fingers, use a
pair of tongs to dip each cutlet in the egg wash.

Figure 7.
Transfer the cutlets or fillets to a pie plate with the bread crumbs
or cornmeal. Press crumbs or cornmeal lightly onto cutlets or
fillets with fingertips to ensure that the crumbs adhere to
the surface of the food.

32

Figure 8.
Transfer the breaded cutlets to a baking rack and allow them to dry for 5 minutes. This drying time stabilizes the breading just enough so that it can be sautéed without sticking to the pan or falling off. Breaded chicken, turkey, and veal cutlets should be handled this way; breaded fish fillets should be cooked as soon as they are breaded.

33

chapter three

TURKEY AND
VEAL CUTLETS

LTHOUGH YOU MAY BE TEMPTED TO COOK turkey cutlets the same way you cook chicken cutlets—don't. Turkey cutlets are much leaner and, more important, much thinner. In our tests, we found that they present the same challenges as veal cutlets.

The biggest risk when preparing ultralean, superthin turkey or veal cutlets is overcooking. Misjudge the timing by a minute or two and this delicate meat can resemble shoe leather. The other major issue is browning. We wondered if turkey and veal cutlets could be cooked in such a way as to promote the development of a crust, one of our favorite things about sautéed chicken cutlets. Could we get these thin cutlets to brown before they overcooked?

On the plus side, there are some factors that make turkey and veal cutlets remarkably easy to prepare. Unlike chicken breasts, these cutlets come in an even thickness, usually about one-quarter inch. There are no tendons or floppy tenderloins to contend with (turkey cutlets are breast slices, not the entire breast half, as is the case with chicken cutlets), and there's no chance that part of the cutlet will overcook while part remains bloody. Also, because the cutlets are so thin, they are a lot less messy to prepare. The fat does not have time to smoke and splatter.

We decided to start our testing with turkey and then see how the final results would work with veal. We began by testing the role of flour. We sautéed two batches of cutlets—one seasoned with just salt and pepper, the other seasoned and then lightly coated on both sides with flour. Although the internal texture of both batches was similar, the exterior was quite different. The floured cutlets developed a light brown crust in places, making a pleasing contrast with the tender, white interior meat. The unfloured cutlets were less flavorful (browning adds flavor), and we missed the crunch added by a nicely browned exterior.

The timing proved remarkably simple—two minutes on the first side and another minute or two on the second.

Once the meat feels firm, take the turkey out of the pan. Use tongs to turn the meat and remove it from the pan. Pricking the meat with a fork can cause juices to escape.

Although most poultry companies put four 4-ounce cutlets in a package and claim that this amount serves four, we find it a bit skimpy. Six cutlets is a more realistic amount for four people. (Serve each person a whole cutlet and cut the remaining two cutlets in half after cooking to yield four more smaller pieces.)

We discovered that veal cutlets can be cooked exactly the same way as turkey cutlets. However, we did encounter some bumps along the road. Most supermarket veal cutlets are improperly butchered, and, as a result, they buckle in the pan and will not brown.

Veal cutlets should be cut from the top round (a cut from the upper portion of the leg). A veal cutlet is a single piece of meat without any muscle separations. When butchered properly, it is cut against the grain so that the surface is perfectly smooth. Butchering the meat against the grain makes the veal especially tender, and its smooth surface permits even browning.

We found that many markets sell cutlets from the shoulder or other parts of the leg. These cutlets are cut with the grain (the surface appears bumpy, indicating the cutlet contains a cross-section of several muscles). This irregular surface buckles when the cutlet is placed in a hot skillet and thus the cutlet will not brown or cook evenly. If you are going to spend the money on veal, we suggest going to a butcher and getting the right cutlets (see figure 9, below) or slicing the cutlets from the top round yourself (see figures 10 and 11, page 38).

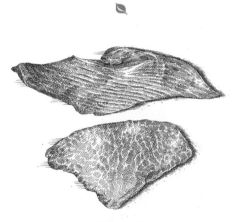

Figure 9.

Veal cutlets should be cut from the top round. Most supermarkets use the leg or sirloin and do not butcher the meat properly—it is cut with the grain, not against the grain, as is best. When shopping, look for cutlets in which no linear striation is evident. The linear striation (in cutlet on top) is an indication that the veal has been cut with the grain and will be tough. Instead, the cutlets should have a smooth surface (like cutlet on bottom) in which no lines are evident.

Figure 10.
To make your own cutlets from a piece of top round, start by
removing the silver skin (the thin white membrane that covers
the meat in places) with a boning knife.

Figure 11.
Once the silver skin has been trimmed, use a long nonflexible
slicing knife to cut slices—on the bias against the grain—that
are between one-quarter and one-half inch thick.

Master Recipe

Sautéed Turkey or Veal Cutlets

serves four

➤ NOTE: *The timing for turkey and veal cutlets is the same. Turkey and veal are fairly bland, so they both match well with aggressively flavored sauces.*

6	turkey or veal cutlets (about 1½ pounds), rinsed and thoroughly dried
	Salt and ground black pepper
½	cup all-purpose flour
2	tablespoons vegetable oil

▦ INSTRUCTIONS:

1. Preheat oven to 200 degrees. Place a plate in oven for keeping cooked cutlets warm while you make one of the pan sauces.

2. Season both sides of cutlets with salt and pepper to taste. Measure flour onto a plate or pie tin. Working with one cutlet at a time, dredge in flour and shake to remove excess.

3. Heat heavy-bottomed 12-inch skillet over high heat until hot, about 4 minutes. Add oil and heat briefly until it shimmers. Lay cutlets in pan. Adjust heat to medium-high (fat should sizzle but not smoke) and sauté cutlets, not moving them until well browned, about 2 minutes. Turn cutlets with tongs and sauté until meat feels firm when pressed, about 1½ minutes. Remove pan from heat and transfer cutlets to warm oven. Continue with one of the variations that follows.

■■ PAN SAUCES:

Marsala Sauce
enough for 4 servings

1	large shallot, minced
12	ounces sliced button mushrooms
1	cup dry Marsala
3	tablespoons unsalted butter, softened
2	teaspoons chopped fresh parsley leaves
	Salt and ground black pepper

Follow Master Recipe for Sautéed Turkey or Veal Cutlets (page 39). Without discarding fat, set skillet over low heat. Add shallot; sauté until softened, about 30 seconds. Increase heat to medium-high, add mushrooms, and sauté until slightly softened, about 30 seconds. Increase heat to high, add Marsala, and scrape skillet bottom with wooden spoon to loosen browned bits. Boil until liquid reduces to about ⅓ cup, 4 to 5 minutes. Add any accumulated meat juices; reduce sauce again to ⅓ cup. Off heat, and swirl in softened butter until it melts and thickens sauce. Add parsley and season with salt and pepper to taste. Spoon sauce over cutlets and serve immediately.

Balsamic and Rosemary Sauce
enough for 4 servings

2	medium garlic cloves, minced
½	cup balsamic vinegar
½	cup dry red wine
1	teaspoon sugar
3	tablespoons unsalted butter, softened
1	teaspoon chopped fresh rosemary
	Salt and ground black pepper

Follow Master Recipe for Sautéed Turkey or Veal Cutlets (page 39). Without discarding fat, set skillet over low heat. Add garlic; sauté until fragrant, about 15 seconds. Increase heat to high, add vinegar, wine, and sugar and scrape skillet bottom with wooden spoon to loosen browned bits. Boil until liquid reduces to about ⅓ cup. Add any accumulated meat juices; reduce sauce again to ⅓ cup. Off heat, and swirl in softened butter until it melts and thickens sauce. Add rosemary and season with salt and pepper to taste. Spoon sauce over cutlets and serve immediately.

Tomato, Pancetta, and Caper Sauce
enough for 4 servings

➤ **NOTE:** *Place diced pancetta (unsmoked Italian bacon) in an empty skillet set over medium-low heat and cook slowly until fat has rendered and pancetta is crisp, about 10 minutes. Transfer pancetta to plate lined with paper towels and reserve until needed.*

1	medium garlic clove, minced
1	cup white wine
½	cup canned diced tomatoes, drained
2	strips lemon peel, about 1 inch long
1	tablespoon capers, rinsed
3	tablespoons unsalted butter, softened
2	teaspoons chopped fresh oregano leaves
	Salt and ground black pepper
2	ounces finely diced pancetta, sautéed until crisp

Follow Master Recipe for Sautéed Turkey or Veal Cutlets (page 39). Without discarding fat, set skillet over low heat. Add garlic; sauté until fragrant, about 15 seconds. Increase heat to high and add wine, tomatoes, lemon peel, and capers and boil until liquid reduces to about ⅓ cup, 4 to 5 minutes, scraping pan bottom with wooden spoon to dislodge browned bits. Add any accumulated meat juices; reduce sauce again to ⅓ cup. Remove lemon peel. Off heat, and swirl in softened butter until it melts and thickens sauce. Add oregano and season with salt and pepper to taste.

Spoon sauce over cutlets, sprinkle with pancetta, and serve immediately.

Olive, Anchovy, and Orange Sauce
enough for 4 servings

2   anchovy fillets, minced
1   medium garlic clove, minced
1   teaspoon grated orange zest
½   cup sweet vermouth
½   cup canned low-sodium chicken broth
⅓   cup pitted and halved oil-cured black olives
3   tablespoons unsalted butter, softened
2   teaspoons fresh chopped basil leaves
     Salt and ground black pepper

Follow Master Recipe for Sautéed Turkey or Veal Cutlets (page 39). Without discarding fat, set skillet over low heat. Add anchovies, garlic, and orange zest; sauté until fragrant, about 15 seconds. Increase heat to high, add vermouth and broth, and boil to reduce to about ⅓ cup, 4 to 5 minutes, scraping pan bottom with wooden spoon to loosen browned bits. Add any accumulated meat juices and reduce sauce again to ⅓ cup. Off heat, and swirl in softened butter until it melts and thickens sauce. Add basil and season with salt and pepper to taste. Spoon sauce over cutlets and serve immediately.

♛

Master Recipe

Sautéed Breaded Turkey or Veal Cutlets

serves four

➤ **NOTE:** *Breaded cutlets need more oil than plain cutlets to brown properly (in this case, ¼ cup) to brown properly. To prevent the coating from burning, keep heat at medium-high. See figures 6–8, pages 32–33, for more information on breading cutlets. Serve with lemon wedges if you like.*

2	large eggs
1	tablespoon water
2	cups bread crumbs, preferably homemade (see page 15)
1	tablespoon chopped fresh parsley leaves
¾	cup all-purpose flour
	Salt and ground black pepper
6	turkey or veal cutlets (about 1½ pounds), rinsed and thoroughly dried
¼	cup vegetable oil

▚ INSTRUCTIONS:

1. Whisk egg with water in a small, flat bowl. Mix bread crumbs and parsley together in pie tin. Measure flour onto a plate or separate pie tin.

2. Season both sides of cutlets with salt and pepper to taste. Working with one cutlet at a time, dredge in flour and shake to remove excess. Using tongs, dip each cutlet into egg wash, letting excess drip off, then place each on bed of crumbs. Press crumbs lightly onto each cutlet with finger-tips to ensure that crumbs adhere to surface of meat. Place breaded cutlets on baking rack to dry for 5 minutes.

3. Heat oil in heavy-bottomed 12-inch skillet over medium-high heat until shimmering, about 2 minutes. Lay cutlets in pan and sauté, not moving them until golden brown, about 2½ minutes. Turn cutlets with tongs and sauté until golden brown, about 2½ minutes more. Serve immediately.

▚ VARIATION:

Sautéed Breaded Turkey or Veal Cutlets with Parmesan

Follow Master Recipe for Breaded Turkey or Veal Cutlets, at left, reducing bread crumbs to 1½ cups and adding ½ cup grated Parmesan cheese to bread crumb mixture.

chapter four

PORK
MEDALLIONS

W E STARTED OUR TESTING WITH THIS basic question: Which part of the pig makes the most sense for a quick weeknight sauté? The two obvious candidates were boneless pork chops and the tenderloin, which we would have to cut into medallions.

We tried a variety of chops, from the loin, rib, and sirloin. While boneless center rib and center loin chops were deemed adequate, we felt that the chops tasted better when cooked with the bone in. In addition, single chops from the loin are cut very thin, and we found that they often dried out when sautéed. Double-thick chops remained moist in our

46

tests, but only when seared and then placed in the oven to cook through. We moved on to the tenderloin.

The tenderloin is a boneless, torpedo-shaped muscle nestled against the rib bones in the loin section, which is roughly equivalent to a position deep inside the midback in a human being. The cut is notable for its remarkable lack of marbling—those ribbons of intramuscular fat that run through meat. While this is a virtue in terms of fat intake, it also presents an obstacle in terms of cooking—that is, the tenderloin is particularly vulnerable to overcooking, which can lead to dry meat. To protect the tenderloin's characteristic tenderness, we prefer to cook it medium-well, so it is slightly rosy inside. This translates into an internal temperature of 145 to 150 degrees. If you prefer your pork well-done and gray-white throughout, this may not be the cut for you.

We proceeded to cut the tenderloin into one-inch slices and pounded them down to three-quarters of an inch with the flat side of a chef's knife (to increase the surface area for searing). We then sautéed them in a bit of sizzling oil for about one minute per side. At the end, every single slice was seared beautifully on both sides, and the pan drippings were perfectly caramelized and ready to deglaze for a flavorful, simple sauce. The whole operation, from refrigerator to table, took only 15 minutes. Beneath the seared crust on each slice was juicy, succulent meat that met all our expectations for this supertender cut.

While testing and retesting our chosen method, we came up with a few pointers to help ensure successful sautéing. First, before cutting the medallions, trim the pearlescent membrane, called the silver skin, from the tenderloin. If left on, the silver skin shrinks in the heat of the pan, pulling the meat up and out of the hot fat, thereby inhibiting browning. Second, do not overcook the meat. There should be just a tinge of pink when you peek into a piece with the tip of a paring knife. The meat will finish cooking as it rests on a plate and you make a pan sauce.

There is one drawback to sautéing a pork tenderloin. Sautéing two batches of medallions, one after the other, in the same pan caused the pan drippings to burn. We found it best to sauté just one large batch of medallions (the pan will be crowded and so must be kept extremely hot).

One tenderloin yields enough medallions for three servings. We have squeezed enough medallions for six servings (from two tenderloins) into one large skillet. If you prefer, cook enough medallions for four people and make a full batch of sauce. The extra few tablespoons of sauce can be used to moisten potatoes or rice.

♛

Master Recipe
Sautéed Pork Tenderloin Medallions
serves six

➤ **NOTE:** *Blot dry the pork medallions with several sheets of paper towel to remove every drop of moisture before cooking, use a 12-inch skillet, and heat the pan until it is blazing hot. Turn the medallions in roughly the same order that they were added to the pan. The side of the medallion that was seared first will develop the best crust and should be presented facing up at the table.*

2	boneless pork tenderloins (about 2 pounds total), trimmed of silver skin (see figure 12, page 50), cut into 1-inch slices, flattened to ¾-inch slices (see figure 13, page 50), and blotted dry with paper towels
	Salt and ground black pepper
2	teaspoons vegetable oil

⁞ INSTRUCTIONS:

1. Heat heavy-bottomed 12-inch skillet over high heat until very hot, about 4 minutes. While skillet is heating, season medallions with salt and pepper to taste.

2. Add oil to pan and swirl to coat bottom. Lay medallions in pan and sauté, not moving them until browned, about 2

minutes. Turn meat with tongs; sauté until firm to the touch, about 1½ minutes. Remove pan from heat, transfer cutlets to a plate, let rest for 5 minutes, then serve immediately.

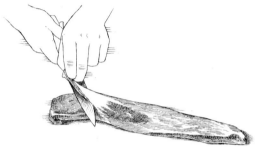

Figure 12.
To remove the silver skin from a pork tenderloin, slip a paring knife between the silver skin and the muscle fibers. Angle the knife upward slightly and use a gentle back-and-forth sawing action.

Figure 13.
A few smacks with the flat side of a chef's knife should flatten the 1-inch slices to a ¾-inch thickness.

Mustard and Tarragon Sauce
enough for 6 servings

1	medium shallot, minced (about 2 tablespoons)
⅓	cup white wine
½	cup canned low-sodium chicken broth
2	tablespoons heavy cream
1	tablespoon Dijon or country mustard
2	teaspoons lemon juice
3	tablespoons unsalted butter, softened
2	teaspoons chopped fresh tarragon leaves
	Salt and ground black pepper

Follow Master Recipe for Sautéed Pork Tenderloin Medallions (page 49). Without discarding fat, set skillet over low heat. Add shallot and sauté until softened slightly, about 30 seconds. Increase heat to high and add wine, broth, and cream, scraping pan bottom with wooden spoon to dislodge browned bits. Boil until liquid reduces to about ⅓ cup, 4 to 5 minutes. Add any accumulated meat juices; reduce again to ⅓ cup. Off heat, swirl in mustard and lemon juice; swirl in softened butter until it melts and thickens sauce. Add tarragon and season with salt and pepper to taste. Spoon sauce over pork and serve immediately.

Asian-Flavored Sauce
with Chile and Star Anise
enough for 6 servings

⅓   cup dry sherry
2½   tablespoons rice wine vinegar
2½   tablespoons soy sauce
3   tablespoons honey
1   tablespoon oyster sauce
2   teaspoons cornstarch
1   teaspoon hot red pepper flakes
2   pods star anise
1   teaspoon Asian sesame oil
1   tablespoon minced fresh gingerroot
1   medium garlic clove, minced

Whisk together sherry, vinegar, soy sauce, honey, oyster sauce, and cornstarch in small bowl; stir in pepper flakes and star anise. Set aside. Follow Master Recipe for Sautéed Pork Tenderloin Medallions (page 49). Without discarding fat, set skillet over low heat. Add sesame oil, ginger, and garlic. Cook until fragrant, about 15 seconds. Increase heat to medium and add sherry mixture, scraping pan bottom with wooden spoon to loosen browned bits; simmer until slightly thickened, about 1 minute. Discard star anise pods before serving. Spoon sauce over pork and serve immediately.

Port Sauce with Dried Cherries and Rosemary
enough for 6 servings

⅓   cup port

½   cup dried cherries

⅔   cup canned low-sodium chicken broth

3   tablespoons unsalted butter, softened

2   teaspoons minced fresh rosemary leaves

    Salt and ground black pepper

Follow Master Recipe for Sautéed Pork Tenderloin Medallions (page 49). Without discarding fat, set skillet over high heat. Add port, cherries, and broth. Boil, scraping pan bottom with wooden spatula to loosen browned bits, until liquid reduces to about ⅓ cup, 4 to 5 minutes. Add any accumulated pork juices; reduce again to ⅓ cup. Off heat, swirl in butter until it melts and thickens sauce. Add rosemary and season with salt and pepper to taste. Spoon sauce over pork and serve immediately.

chapter five

STEAK

OUR IDEAL STEAK IS ONE COOKED IN SUCH A way that the entire surface caramelizes and forms a rich, thick crust—in other words, it is grilled. The intense heat of the grill makes it easy to obtain such a crust. But what about when the weather makes grilling impractical? We wanted to get the same result from sautéing.

This task turned out to be harder than we imagined. Sometimes we did get the great crust we were looking for, but sometimes we didn't. We needed to figure out which cuts of steak and what cooking technique were best suited to sautéing.

It quickly became clear that boneless steaks are a must when sautéing. The bone in a T-bone or porterhouse steak protrudes slightly above the meat. When grilling, this slightly thicker bone makes no difference in cooking because the meat can sag slightly between the open wrungs on the rack. When sautéing, this does not happen. The bone remains in contact with the pan but the meat remains slightly elevated above the solid pan surface. The result is poor browning.

A boneless steak comes into direct contact with the pan and browns much more easily. We found that our favorite steaks on the grill—the strip and the rib (see figure 14, page 57)—worked equally well in a hot skillet as long as we chose boneless versions. We wondered, though, if any cheaper cuts would work. On the grill, we like to cook shoulder steak cut for London broil and flank steak. However, these long pieces of meat are not suited to sautéing—they don't fit in a round skillet. We needed smaller, individual steaks that looked like the strip or rib steak.

We tested top and bottom round, the cuts many sources suggest for cooks on a budget. The top round was tough and bland. The bottom round had a better flavor, but the texture was equally tough. Our butcher recommended top sirloin as well as boneless top butt, or rump, steaks. Although these steaks cost about as much as the round, we found them to be more flavorful and less chewy. At half the price of rib-eye and strip steak, the top sirloin offers an excellent value (see figure 15, right).

With our cuts of meat chosen, we started to refine our technique. It was obvious to us from the beginning that the key to browning the steaks was going to be preheating the pan, so that when the steaks hit, the surface it would be hot enough to sear the meat before it had a chance to overcook. (We also found out the hard way that the steak may stick if the pan isn't well heated, leaving the delicious seared flavor in the pan, not the steak.)

We sautéed steaks in two tablespoons, one tablespoon, two teaspoons, and one teaspoon of oil. Since all of our preferred cuts of steaks give off some fat as they cook, we found that one teaspoon was adequate and kept the splattering to a minimum.

We wondered if a combination of high and medium heat would deliver the best results—browning the exterior and then allowing the interior to cook through. We found that constant high heat delivers the best-looking and best-tasting crust. Although the interior is a bit underdone when the steak comes out of the pan, a five-minute rest lets the interior finish cooking and allows the juices to be redistributed evenly throughout the meat.

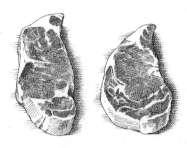

Figure 14.

The finest steaks for sautéing—though costly—are unquestionably the boneless strip steak (left) and boneless rib-eye steak (right). The strip, also called the shell, top loin, or New York strip, is moderately chewy and has a noticeable grain. The flavor is excellent. The rib eye (also called a rib steak) is very tender and smooth-textured, with a distinctive beefy taste that is robust and rich. There are also pockets of fat in this cut, while the strip steak is a bit leaner.

Figure 15.

Our first pick for a delicious, less expensive steak for sautéing is the top sirloin steak, also called sirloin butt, or rump, steak. At about $5.50 per pound, this steak offers excellent flavor and value and is very tender.

Master Recipe

Sautéed Steak

serves four

➤ **NOTE:** *Our favorite steaks for this recipe are the strip and the rib. If you don't want to pay top dollar, try top sirloin. It will be a bit chewier and not quite as buttery, but still quite good.*

4   boneless 8-ounce beef steaks, 1 to 1¼ inches
    thick, thoroughly dried with paper towels
    Salt and ground black pepper
1   teaspoon vegetable oil

INSTRUCTIONS:

1. Heat heavy-bottomed, 12-inch skillet over high heat until very hot, about 4 minutes. While skillet is heating, season steaks with salt and pepper to taste.

2. Add oil to pan; swirl to coat bottom. Lay steaks in pan and sauté, not moving them until well browned, about 4 minutes. Turn meat with tongs; sauté 3 minutes more for rare, 4 minutes for medium-rare, and 5 minutes for medium. Remove pan from heat and transfer steaks to a plate and let rest 5 minutes, or while making sauce, then serve immediately. If using compound butter, place a pat of butter on top of each steak and let rest for about 2 minutes, then serve immediately.

58

Red Wine Sauce
enough for 4 servings

2 medium shallots, minced
2 teaspoons brown sugar
½ cup dry red wine
½ cup canned low-sodium chicken broth
½ bay leaf
1 tablespoon balsamic vinegar
3 tablespoons unsalted butter, softened
1 teaspoons chopped fresh thyme leaves
Salt and ground black pepper

Follow Master Recipe for Sautéed Steak (at left). Without discarding fat, set skillet over low heat. Add shallots and brown sugar and sauté until shallots are softened slightly, about 30 seconds. Increase heat to high and add wine, broth, and bay leaf, scraping pan bottom with wooden spoon to dislodge browned bits. Boil until liquid reduces to about ⅓ cup, 4 to 5 minutes. Add vinegar and any accumulated meat juices; reduce again to ⅓ cup. Off heat, swirl in softened butter until it melts and thickens sauce. Add thyme and season with salt and pepper to taste. Spoon sauce over steaks and serve immediately.

Brandy Peppercorn Sauce
enough for 4 servings

3	tablespoons black peppercorns, very coarsely ground
	Salt
2	medium shallots, minced
½	cup brandy or cognac
½	cup canned low-sodium chicken broth
¼	cup heavy cream
	Pinch ground cloves
3	tablespoons unsalted butter, softened
2	teaspoons chopped fresh parsley leaves or chives
1	teaspoon lemon juice

While pan is heating, dry steaks well, press peppercorns into both sides of meat, and sprinkle with salt. Follow Master Recipe for Sautéed Steak (page 58). Without discarding fat, set skillet over low heat. Add shallots and sauté until slightly softened, about 30 seconds. Increase heat to high, add brandy, broth, cream, and cloves and boil until liquid reduces to about ⅓ cup, scraping pan bottom with wooden spoon to loosen browned bits. Add any accumulated juices; reduce sauce again to ⅓ cup. Off heat, swirl in softened butter until it melts and thickens sauce. Add parsley or chives and lemon juice and season with salt to taste. Spoon sauce over steaks and serve immediately.

Steak Diane
enough for 4 servings

2	large shallots, minced
½	cup brandy or cognac
½	cup canned low-sodium chicken broth
1	tablespoon Dijon mustard
1	tablespoon lemon juice
1	tablespoon Worcestershire sauce
3	tablespoons unsalted butter, softened
2	teaspoons minced fresh chives
	Salt and ground black pepper

Follow Master Recipe for Sautéed Steak (page 58). Without discarding fat, set skillet over low heat. Add shallots and sauté until softened slightly, about 30 seconds. Increase heat to high, add brandy and broth and boil until liquid reduces to about ⅓ cup, scraping pan bottom with wooden spoon to loosen browned bits. Add mustard, lemon juice, and Worcestershire sauce and any accumulated juices; reduce sauce again to ⅓ cup. Off heat, swirl in softened butter until it melts and thickens sauce. Add chives and season with salt and pepper to taste. Spoon sauce over steaks and serve immediately.

Dried Porcini and Rosemary Sauce
enough for 4 servings

½   ounce dried porcini mushrooms

½   cup hot water

2   medium garlic cloves, minced

⅓   cup dry vermouth

⅓   cup canned low-sodium chicken broth

3   tablespoons unsalted butter, softened

2   teaspoons chopped fresh rosemary

Salt and ground black pepper

INSTRUCTIONS:

1. Soak dried mushrooms in hot water for 30 minutes. Remove mushrooms and cut into 1-inch lengths. Pour remaining liquid through strainer lined with coffee filter or several layers of cheesecloth; reserve liquid.

2. Follow Master Recipe for Sautéed Steak (page 58). Without discarding fat, set skillet over low heat. Add garlic and sauté until fragrant, about 15 seconds. Increase heat to high, add porcini and their liquid, vermouth, and broth and boil to reduce to about ⅓ cup, scraping pan with spoon to loosen brown bits. Add accumulated juices and reduce again to ⅓ cup. Off heat, swirl in softened butter until it melts and thickens sauce. Add rosemary and season with salt and pepper to taste. Spoon sauce over steaks and serve immediately.

Compound Butters for Sautéed Steak
enough for 4 steaks

➤ **NOTE:** *You can double or triple any of these recipes and store extra butter in the freezer. If making a large batch of compound butter, use a standing mixer to combine the ingredients evenly.*

Rosemary-Parmesan Butter

4	tablespoons unsalted butter, softened
3	tablespoons grated Parmesan cheese
2	teaspoons chopped fresh rosemary
1	small garlic clove, minced
⅛	teaspoon hot red pepper flakes
⅛	teaspoon salt

Roquefort Butter

4	tablespoons unsalted butter, softened
3	tablespoons crumbled Roquefort cheese
2	teaspoons minced fresh sage leaves
1	teaspoon minced fresh parsley leaves
1	medium shallot, minced
2	teaspoons port
	Pinch ground black pepper
⅛	teaspoon salt

Tapenade Butter

4	tablespoons unsalted butter, softened
1	teaspoon minced fresh thyme leaves
1	small garlic clove, minced (about 1 teaspoon)
⅛	teaspoon finely grated orange zest
½	anchovy fillet, minced
10	pitted and finely chopped oil-cured black olives (about 2 tablespoons)
1½	teaspoons brandy
	Pinch ground black pepper
⅛	teaspoon salt

⋮⋮ INSTRUCTIONS:

1. Beat butter with large fork until light and fluffy. Add remaining ingredients and mix to combine.

2. As shown in figure 16 (right), roll butter into a log about 3 inches long and 1½ inches in diameter. Refrigerate until firm, at least 2 hours and up to 3 days. (Butter can be frozen for 2 months. When ready to use, let soften just until butter can be cut, about 15 minutes.)

3. To use, remove compound butter from refrigerator and slice into 4 pieces just before sautéing steaks. Place one piece on each steak just as it comes out of the pan (see figure 17, right). Let rest for 2 minutes and serve immediately.

Figure 16.
Compound butters are a great way to add flavor to a cooked steak. Once the ingredients have been combined, place the butter mixture in the center of a piece of plastic wrap. Fold one edge of the plastic wrap over the butter. Glide your hands back and forth over the butter to shape it into a 3-inch cylinder. Twist the ends of the plastic wrap shut and refrigerate until firm.

Figure 17.
When ready to use, unwrap the butter and cut it into 4 equal pieces. Place each piece on top of a just-cooked steak.

65

chapter six

∋

FISH FILLETS
AND STEAKS

W E WANTED TO ESTABLISH A CONSIS-
tent method for cooking fish. While
most fish must be cooked in a blazing
hot pan to promote browning, we
quickly realized that a thick salmon fillet with skin on could
not be treated like a thin, skinless piece of flounder.

After much testing, we eventually divided boneless fish
into three categories: white-fleshed fillets (everything from
sole and flounder to cod and snapper), steaks (tuna and
swordfish), and salmon fillets (which have their own unique
cooking challenges). We developed a number of sauces that
work well with all three classes of fish. The cooking issues,
however, are distinct. Here are our findings.

66

When sautéing very thin fillets, first make sure that your pan can properly accommodate the fish. The fillets should lie flat and uncrowded in the pan. In our testing, if a piece of fish snuck up the cooler, ungreased side of the pan, it stuck and fell apart when flipped over. Because some flat fish fillets can be quite large, it is better to cut them before cooking so they lie flat. Another trick you can use to fit fillets that taper down to a thin tail and to avoid overcooking the thinner portion is to fold the tail over the main portion of the fillet so the piece is all of the same thickness.

To keep the fillets from sticking, shake the pan occasionally before flipping them. If a fillet does stick, don't scrape it off the bottom of the pan; instead, let it cook a bit longer. We found that most often the fish sticks because it hasn't had a chance to form its protective crust. Once the crust is formed, it will shake loose.

Once you turn the fillets, really thin pieces (less than ½ inch thick) will finish cooking by absorbing the residual heat in the pan, so turn off the heat source. Thicker fillets need more time, but we found it best to turn the heat to medium-high to lessen splattering and prevent scorching.

To see if the fish is done, poke it with your finger. It should feel firm but not flake. If the fish falls into dry flakes, it has been overcooked.

Sautéing thick fish steaks raises different issues. Tuna and swordfish steaks are usually sold in large, 16-ounce pieces that can be hard to cook evenly. By the time the heat reaches the center, the edges have overcooked. Cutting the steaks in half minimizes this problem. Even with steaks that were one inch thick, we found that the heat distributed more evenly through narrower pieces. An 8-ounce steak also makes an ideal single serving.

While we found that white fish fillets benefited from a dusting of flour, which helped them brown and produced a nice thick crust, we found that steaks were better left unfloured. The sturdy nature of the flesh and the longer cooking time encourage plenty of browning.

With its skin on, salmon raises other issues. We wondered if it needed as much fat. We started with two tablespoons— the amount we used to sauté white fish fillets. The results were greasy. We then cut back to one tablespoon—the amount we used to sauté tuna and salmon steaks. We thought there was too much splattering. Eventually, we found that one teaspoon of fat is sufficient to cook four salmon fillets.

As with other pieces of fish, we preheated the pan until it was very hot and tried cooking over high heat. Billows of smoke soon filled the kitchen. We found that preheating on high was fine but that the heat had to be turned down to medium-high once the fish was added to the pan.

♛

Master Recipe

Sautéed Thin Fish Fillets

serves four

➤ **NOTE:** *Thin fish fillets measure between ¼ inch and ½ inch thick and include flounder, sole, and catfish. Longer fillets can cook unevenly. Folding over the thin end of the fillet not only facilitates even cooking but also enables you to fit all the fillets in the pan at one time.*

1½   pounds thin fish fillets, skinned (see figure 18, page 71), rinsed, and dried with paper towels (about 5 to 7 fillets, depending on thickness)
      Salt and ground black pepper

¾   cup all-purpose flour

2   tablespoons vegetable oil

⠿ INSTRUCTIONS:

1. Heat oven to 200 degrees. Place plate in oven for keeping cooked fillets warm while you make sauce.

2. Sprinkle fillets with salt and pepper to taste. Measure flour onto a plate or pie tin. Working with one fillet at a time, dredge with flour and shake to remove excess. Fold thin tail over meaty portion of fillet (see figure 19, page 71).

69

3. Heat heavy-bottomed, 12-inch skillet over high heat until very hot, about 4 minutes. Add oil, lay fillets in pan, and sauté, shaking pan occasionally to keep fillets from sticking (see figure 20, page 73), until golden brown, 2 to 3 minutes. Turn fish with spatula. If fillets are very thin (about ¼ inch), turn heat off immediately, allowing residual heat from pan to finish cooking fish. If fish is a little thicker (about ½ inch), continue to cook over medium-high heat for 1 more minute. Remove pan from heat and transfer fillets to warm oven while making sauce.

▓ VARIATION:

Sautéed Thick Fish Fillets

Thick fish fillets measure between ¾ inch and 1 inch thick and include fish like striped bass, red snapper, grouper, and haddock. There's no need to fold over the ends of the fillets here; they are not very thin.

Follow Master Recipe for Sautéed Thin Fish Fillets (page 69), cooking 1½ pounds thick fillets (4 to 6 pieces, depending on thickness) on first side until golden brown, 3 to 4 minutes. Cook on second side for 2 to 3 minutes more.

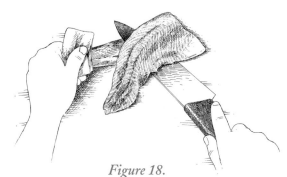

Figure 18.
To more easily remove the skin from a fish fillet, start at the end
of the tail, then slide your knife along between the skin and flesh
of the tail until you can grab hold of the skin with a paper towel.
Use this "handle" to help separate the skin from the flesh.

Figure 19.
When sautéing fish fillets that taper down to a thin tail, fold the
tail over the fillet to ensure even cooking. Because the pan will be
quite hot, it's best to do this on the cutting board. Be sure that the
sauté pan you use is large enough to comfortably hold the fillets in
a single layer without overcrowding.

71

♛

Master Recipe

Sautéed Fish Steaks

serves four

➤ **NOTE:** *This method works well for steak-type fish such as swordfish and tuna. If you like your fish rare in the middle, make sure to cook it according to the lowest time given. It is imperative that the skillet be extremely hot to prevent sticking. Most markets sell 1-inch steaks that weigh about 1 pound. At home, cut these pieces in half before cooking to yield individual portions.*

4   fish steaks (each about 8 ounces and ¾ inch to
     1 inch thick), rinsed and dried with paper towels
     Salt and ground black pepper
1   tablespoon vegetable oil

▓ **INSTRUCTIONS:**

1. Turn oven to 200 degrees. Place plate in oven for keeping cooked steaks warm while you make sauce.

2. Heat heavy-bottomed, 12-inch skillet over high heat until very hot, about 4 minutes. While pan is heating, sprinkle fish with salt and pepper to taste.

3. Add oil and swirl to coat pan bottom. Lay steaks in pan and sauté, shaking pan occasionally to keep steaks from sticking, until golden, 1 to 1½ minutes. Turn steaks with spatula and continue sautéing on second side until just cooked to preference, 1 to 1½ minutes more. Remove pan from heat and transfer steaks to warm oven while making sauce.

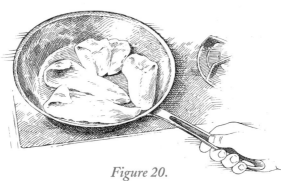

Figure 20.
Fish fillets and steaks are prone to sticking. As they cook, slide the skillet across the burner by quickly moving your wrist back and forth. Don't shake the pan so violently that the fish moves up the sides of the skillet.

73

Master Recipe

Sautéed Salmon Fillets

serves four

➤ **NOTE:** *Because salmon fillets are thicker than other fillets, they must be cooked on medium-high heat (not high heat) so that the exterior doesn't burn before the interior cooks through. With the addition of the fish, the pan temperature drops; compensate for the heat loss by keeping the heat on high for 30 seconds after adding them, then turn down the heat.*

4   skin-on salmon fillets (each about 6 ounces and 1 to 1¼ inches thick), rinsed and dried with paper towels
      Salt and ground black pepper
1   teaspoon vegetable oil

INSTRUCTIONS:

1. Heat oven to 200 degrees. Place plate in oven for keeping cooked fillets warm while you make sauce.

2. Heat heavy-bottomed, 12-inch skillet over high heat until very hot, about 4 minutes. Sprinkle salmon with salt and pepper to taste.

3. Add oil to pan; swirl to coat. Add fillets skin-side down and cook, without moving fish, until pan regains lost heat, about 30 seconds. Reduce heat to medium-high; continue to cook until skin side is well browned, about 4½ minutes. Turn fillets and cook, without moving them, until they are no longer translucent on the exterior and are firm, but not hard, when gently squeezed, 3 minutes for medium-rare, 3½ minutes for medium. Remove pan from heat and transfer fillets to warm oven while making sauce.

▓ PAN SAUCES:

The following sauces can be used with thin or thick fillets as well as fish steaks and salmon fillets.

Balsamic Basil Sauce
enough for 4 servings

1	tablespoon sugar
1	large shallot, minced
⅓	cup balsamic vinegar
½	cup bottled clam juice
1	small tomato, peeled, cored, seeded, and cut into ½-inch dice (about ½ cup)
3	tablespoons unsalted butter, softened
2	teaspoons chopped fresh basil leaves
	Salt and ground black pepper

Follow a Master Recipe to cook fish (pages 69–75). Without discarding fat, set skillet over low heat. Sprinkle sugar into skillet; cook, without stirring, until sugar is golden brown, about 1 minute. Add shallot; sauté until softened slightly, about 30 seconds. Increase heat to high, add vinegar, clam juice, and tomato, scraping pan bottom with wooden spoon to loosen brown bits. Boil until reduced to ⅓ cup, 4 to 5 minutes. Add any accumulated juices and reduce sauce again to ⅓ cup. Remove from heat, swirl in butter until it melts and thickens sauce. Add basil and season with salt and pepper to taste. Spoon sauce over fish and serve immediately.

Chipotle Orange Sauce
enough for 4 servings

1	tablespoon sugar
2	medium garlic cloves, minced
2	small chipotle chiles en adobo, minced (about 2 teaspoons)
⅓	cup balsamic vinegar
½	cup orange juice
3	tablespoons unsalted butter, softened
2	teaspoons chopped fresh cilantro leaves
	Salt and ground black pepper

Follow a Master Recipe to cook fish (pages 69–75). Without discarding fat, set skillet over low heat. Sprinkle sugar into skillet; cook, without stirring, until sugar is golden brown, about 1 minute. Add garlic and chipotles, and sauté until fragrant, about 10 seconds. Increase heat to high, add vinegar and orange juice, and boil until sauce is reduced to ⅓ cup, 4 to 5 minutes, scraping pan bottom with wooden spoon to loosen brown bits. Add any accumulated fish juices and reduce sauce again to ⅓ cup. Remove pan from heat, swirl in softened butter until it melts and thickens sauce. Add cilantro and season with salt and pepper to taste. Spoon sauce over fish and serve immediately.

Fresh Tomato and Rosemary Sauce
enough for 4 servings

1	large shallot, minced
½	cup dry white wine
⅓	cup bottled clam juice
1	small tomato, peeled, cored, seeded, and cut into ½ -inch dice (about ½ cup)
3	tablespoons unsalted butter, softened
1	teaspoon chopped fresh rosemary
	Salt and ground black pepper

Follow a Master Recipe to cook fish (pages 69–75). Without discarding fat, set skillet over low heat. Add shallot; sauté until softened slightly, about 30 seconds. Increase heat to high, add wine and clam juice, and boil until sauce is reduced to ⅓ cup, 4 to 5 minutes, scraping skillet bottom with wooden spoon to loosen browned bits. Add tomato and any accumulated fish juices and reduce sauce again to ⅓ cup. Remove pan from heat and swirl in butter until melted and sauce is thickened. Add rosemary and season with salt and pepper to taste. Spoon sauce over fish and serve immediately.

Lemon-Parsley Sauce with Capers
enough for 4 servings

1	large shallot, minced
⅓	cup dry white wine
½	cup bottled clam juice
2	tablespoons lemon juice
1	tablespoon capers, rinsed
2	pieces lemon peel, each 1 inch square
3	tablespoons unsalted butter, softened
2	teaspoons chopped fresh parsley leaves
	Salt and ground black pepper

Follow a Master Recipe to cook fish (pages 69–75). Without discarding fat, set skillet over low heat. Add shallot; sauté until softened slightly, about 30 seconds. Increase heat to high, add wine, clam juice, lemon juice, capers, and lemon peel, scraping pan bottom with wooden spoon to loosen browned bits. Boil until sauce is reduced to ⅓ cup, 4 to 5 minutes. Add any accumulated fish juices and reduce sauce again to ⅓ cup. Remove pan from heat and swirl in softened butter until it melts and thickens sauce. Remove lemon peel, add parsley, and season with salt and pepper to taste. Spoon over fish and serve immediately.

Mustard Dill Sauce
enough for 4 servings

1	large shallot, minced
½	cup dry white wine
½	cup bottled clam juice
1	tablespoon Dijon mustard
3	tablespoons unsalted butter, softened
2	teaspoons chopped fresh dill
	Salt and ground black pepper

Follow a Master Recipe to cook fish (pages 69–75). Without discarding fat, set skillet over low heat. Add shallot; sauté until softened slightly, about 30 seconds. Increase heat to high, add wine and clam juice, and boil until sauce is reduced to ⅓ cup, 4 to 5 minutes, scraping pan bottom with wooden spoon to loosen brown bits. Add any accumulated fish juices and reduce sauce again to ⅓ cup. Remove pan from heat and stir in mustard. Swirl in softened butter until it melts and thickens sauce. Add dill and season with salt and pepper to taste. Spoon sauce over fish and serve immediately.

♔

Master Recipe

Sautéed Breaded Fish Fillets

serves four

➤ **NOTE:** *Bread crumbs can turn soggy on moist fish fillets. We found that cornmeal makes a crisper coating. You can't tuck the ends of breaded fillets under because they won't brown. Therefore, you will need to sauté the breaded fillets in two batches or use two 12-inch skillets. Refer to figures 6 through 8 on pages 32 and 33 for hints on breading fillets. Don't sauce breaded fillets or they will become soggy. Instead, serve with lemon wedges, garlic or herb mayonnaise, or tartar sauce.*

2	large eggs, lightly beaten
1	tablespoon water
¾	cup all-purpose flour
1	cup cornmeal
1½	pounds thin fish fillets, skinned (see figure 18, page 71), rinsed, and dried with paper towels (about 5 to 7 fillets, depending on thickness)
	Salt and ground black pepper
½	cup vegetable oil

▦ **INSTRUCTIONS:**

1. Turn oven to 200 degrees. Place plate in oven for keeping cooked fillets warm while you prepare second batch.

80

2. Whisk egg with water in small, flat bowl. Measure flour and cornmeal onto separate pie tins.

3. Season fillets with salt and pepper to taste, then dredge them one at a time in flour, knocking off excess. Using tongs, dip each fillet into egg wash, letting excess drip off, then place each on bed of cornmeal. Press cornmeal lightly onto fillets with fingertips to ensure that it adheres to surface of fish.

4. Heat heavy-bottomed, 12-inch skillet over high heat until very hot, about 4 minutes. Add ¼ cup oil, lay half the fillets in pan, and sauté, shaking pan occasionally to keep fillets from sticking, until golden brown, 1½ to 2 minutes. Turn fish with spatula and continue sautéing on second side until golden, 1 to 2 minutes more. Transfer to plate in oven. Repeat process with remaining oil and fillets. Serve immediately.

chapter seven

SHRIMP AND SCALLOPS

SAUTÉING SHRIMP POSES A NUMBER OF PROB-
lems. Overcooking will produce shrimp reminiscent of rubber, but shrimp cooked too little
will have a mushy texture. Shrimp retains a lot
of water, and it often steams while cooking instead of main-
taining a steady sauté.

Given our general success of starting with a hot pan
when sautéing, we cooked several batches of shrimp this
way. High heat helped somewhat in our quest to keep the
shrimp from steaming, but not enough. We ended up
sautéing the shrimp in two batches, allowing the pan to hold
its heat at a more consistent level. Cooking in batches also

reduced the chances of overcooking the shrimp. Initially, we had too many shrimp to turn in too short a time; those placed in the pan at the beginning were rock-solid by the time the last shrimp was flipped.

We found that precise timing is the key to perfectly cooked shrimp. A few seconds made the difference between shrimp that was succulent or just barely edible. Jumbo shrimp allowed for a slightly larger margin of error in terms of cooking time than medium or large shrimp. There are no industry standards for sizing shrimp. Since all the terms are relative, buy shrimp according to the number it takes to make a pound. Shrimp labeled "16/20," for example, require 16 to 20 individual pieces to make a pound.

Once shrimp are purchased, they must be prepared for cooking. When sautéing, we found it best to peel the shrimp before cooking. (In contrast, shells protect shrimp when grilling.) Sautéed shrimp are always sauced, and it's much too hard to eat sauced shrimp that have their shells on. In addition, the shells prevent the sauce from flavoring the shrimp meat.

Shrimp preparation also raises the issue of deveining, which generates much controversy, even among experts. Although some people won't eat shrimp that has not been deveined, others believe that the "vein"—actually, the animal's intestinal tract—contributes flavor and insist on leaving it in. In our tests, we could not detect an effect (either positive or negative) on flavor when we left the vein in. The vein is generally so tiny in most medium-sized shrimp that it virtually disappears after cooking. Out of laziness, we leave it alone. In very large shrimp, the vein is usually larger as well. Very large veins can detract from the overall texture of the shrimp and are best removed before cooking.

Instead of using the more bountiful sauces that we developed for the other chapters in this book, we found that shrimp are best sauced with a concentrated glaze—something that can adhere to the shrimp. Scallops also work best with a glaze. Because the shrimp and scallop sauces are interchangeable, we are covering both kinds of shellfish here, in one chapter.

Without a doubt, sautéing is the best way to cook scallops. The high heat caramelizes the exterior to form a concentrated, nutty flavored crust. The caramelized exterior enhances the natural sweetness of the scallop and provides a nice, crisp contrast with the tender interior.

Unfortunately, many scallops are watery and steam rather than sauté when cooked in a hot pan. That's because most scallops (by some estimates up to 90 percent of the retail supply) are dipped in a phosphate and water mixture to extend their shelf life. During processing, scallops absorb water, which is then thrown off when they are cooked. You can't brown processed scallops in a skillet.

By law, processed scallops must be identified at the wholesale level, so ask your fishmonger. Also, look at the scallops. Scallops are naturally ivory or pinkish tan; processing turns them bright white. Processed scallops are slippery and swollen, and they usually sit in milky white liquid at the store. Unprocessed scallops (also called dry scallops) are sticky and flabby. If they are surrounded by any liquid (and often they are not), the juices are clear, not white.

As for the type of scallop, we found large sea scallops to be the best choice when sautéing. Because they can be left in the pan longer than small bay or calico scallops, they are better able to brown without overcooking.

To preserve the creamy texture of the flesh, we cooked the scallops to medium-rare, which means the scallop is hot all the way through but that the center still retains some translucence. As a scallop cooks, the soft flesh firms and you can see an opaqueness develop, starting at the bottom of the scallop, where it sits in the pan, and then slowly creeping up toward the center. The scallop is medium-rare when the sides have firmed up and all but about the middle third of the scallop has turned opaque.

Scallops will continue to cook via residual heat as they wait to be sauced, so don't hesitate to pull scallops from the pan when they look a bit underdone.

Master Recipe
Sautéed Shrimp
serves four

➤ **NOTE:** *This recipe requires quick work. The shrimp can be dumped into the pan and spread in a single layer by shaking the skillet. For even cooking, you must turn each shrimp individually. To make this as easy as possible, we recommend buying large shrimp and using a pair of tongs.*

1 tablespoon vegetable oil
2 pounds large shrimp (16 to 20 per pound),
    peeled, deveined if desired, rinsed, and
    thoroughly dried
    Salt and ground black pepper

INSTRUCTIONS:

1. Turn oven to 200 degrees. Place plate in oven to keep shrimp warm while making second batch and sauce.

2. Heat heavy-bottomed, 12-inch skillet over high heat until very hot, about 4 minutes. Add 1½ teaspoons oil to pan; swirl to coat bottom. Add half the shrimp and sauté until bottoms are just pink, about 45 seconds to 1 minute. Turn shrimp with tongs (see figure 21, right). Sauté until shrimp are just cooked and pink all over, 1 to 1½ minutes.

Remove pan from heat and transfer shrimp to warm oven while cooking remaining shrimp.

3. Let pan return to temperature over high heat for 10 to 15 seconds. Add remaining 1½ teaspoons oil, swirl to coat bottom of pan, then add remaining shrimp and cook as directed in step 2. Transfer shrimp to warm oven while making sauce.

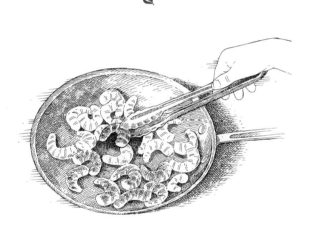

Figure 21.
To cook evenly, shrimp must be turned once as they become pink. We found that a using a pair of tongs—although tedious—is the only way to ensure that all the shrimp are actually turned. Work as quickly as possible to make sure that all of the shrimp are cooking at the same rate.

♛

Master Recipe

Sautéed Scallops

serves four

➤ **NOTE:** *This recipe was developed for standard sea scallops, which are about the size of a short, squat marshmallow. If using smaller scallops, turn off the heat as soon as you turn them; they will finish cooking from the residual heat, 15 to 30 seconds longer.*

1	tablespoon vegetable oil
1½	pounds sea scallops (about 30 to a pound), small muscles removed (see figure 22, right)
	Salt and ground black pepper

INSTRUCTIONS:

1. Turn oven to 200 degrees. Place plate in oven to keep scallops warm while making second batch and sauce.

2. Heat heavy-bottomed, 12-inch skillet over high heat until very hot, about 4 minutes. Add 1½ teaspoons oil; swirl to coat bottom. Add half the scallops, one at a time, flat side down. Season with salt and pepper to taste. Cook until scallops are well browned, 1½ to 2 minutes. Using tongs, turn scallops, one at a time. Cook until medium-rare (sides have firmed up and all but middle third of scallop is opaque), 30 to 90 seconds longer, depending on size. Remove pan from

88

heat and transfer scallops to warm oven while cooking remaining scallops.

3. Let pan return to temperature over high heat for 10 to 15 seconds. Add remaining 1½ teaspoons oil, swirl to coat bottom of pan, then add remaining scallops and cook as directed in step 2. Transfer scallops to warm oven while making sauce.

Figure 22.

The small, rough-textured, crescent-shaped muscle that attaches the scallop to the shell is often not removed during processing. You can readily remove any muscles that are still attached. If you don't, they will toughen slightly during cooking.

▦ PAN SAUCES:

These sauces—really more like glazes because they are so concentrated—can be used with shrimp or scallops.

Garlic, White Wine, and Lemon Sauce
enough for 4 servings

4	medium garlic cloves, minced
½	cup dry white wine
2	tablespoons lemon juice
3	tablespoons unsalted butter, softened
2	teaspoons chopped fresh parsley leaves
	Salt and ground black pepper

Follow Master Recipe for Sautéed Shrimp (page 86) or Scallops (page 88). Without discarding fat, set skillet over low heat. Add garlic to pan; sauté until fragrant, about 15 seconds. Increase heat to high, add wine and lemon juice, scraping pan bottom with wooden spoon to loosen brown bits. Boil until sauce liquid is reduced to 3 tablespoons, 3 to 4 minutes. Add any accumulated seafood juices and reduce sauce again to 3 tablespoons, cooking about 1 minute more. Remove pan from heat and swirl in butter until it melts and thickens sauce. Add parsley and season with salt and pepper to taste. Add shrimp or scallops to sauce, toss, and serve immediately.

Cuban Citrus Glaze
enough for 4 servings

2	medium garlic cloves, minced
¾	teaspoon ground cumin
¼	cup orange juice
¼	cup lime juice
3	tablespoons unsalted butter, softened
2	teaspoons chopped fresh oregano leaves
	Salt and ground black pepper

Follow Master Recipe for Sautéed Shrimp (page 86) or Scallops (page 88). Without discarding fat, set skillet over low heat. Add garlic and cumin, sauté until fragrant, about 15 seconds. Increase heat to high, add orange juice and lime juice. Boil until sauce liquid is reduced to 3 tablespoons, 3 to 4 minutes. Add any accumulated seafood juices and reduce sauce again to 3 tablespoons, cooking about 1 minute more. Remove pan from heat and swirl in butter until it melts and thickens sauce. Add oregano and season with salt and pepper to taste. Add shrimp or scallops to sauce, toss, and serve immediately.

Curried Tomato Sauce with Basil
enough for 4 servings

2	medium garlic cloves, minced
1½	teaspoons curry powder
1	teaspoon sugar
½	cup dark beer
1	cup halved cherry tomatoes
3	tablespoons unsalted butter, softened
2	teaspoons thinly sliced fresh basil leaves
	Salt and ground black pepper

Follow Master Recipe for Sautéed Shrimp (page 86) or Scallops (page 88). Without discarding fat, set skillet over low heat. Add garlic, curry, and sugar; sauté until fragrant, about 15 seconds. Increase heat to high and add beer, scraping bottom of pan with wooden spoon to loosen brown bits. Boil until sauce liquid is reduced to 3 tablespoons, 3 to 4 minutes. Add any accumulated seafood juices and reduce sauce again to 3 tablespoons, about 1 minute more. Remove pan from heat, add tomatoes, and swirl in butter until it melts and thickens sauce. Add basil and season with salt and pepper to taste. Add shrimp or scallops to sauce, toss, and serve immediately.

Lemon-Vodka Glaze

enough for 4 servings

1	medium shallot, minced
2	teaspoons fennel seeds
½	cup vodka
2	strips lemon peel, about 2 inches long
1	tablespoon lemon juice
3	tablespoons unsalted butter, softened
2	teaspoons chopped fresh parsley leaves
	Salt and ground black pepper

Follow Master Recipe for Sautéed Shrimp (page 86) or Scallops (page 88). Without discarding fat, set skillet over low heat. Add shallot and fennel seeds, sauté until shallots are softened slightly, about 30 seconds. Increase heat to high, remove pan from heat, add vodka, lemon peel, and lemon juice. Return pan to heat, scraping pan bottom with wooden spoon to loosen brown bits. Boil until sauce liquid is reduced to 3 tablespoons, 3 to 4 minutes. Add any accumulated seafood juices and reduce sauce again to 3 tablespoons, about 1 minute more. Remove pan from heat and swirl in butter until it melts and thickens sauce. Remove lemon peel, add parsley, and season with salt and pepper to taste. Add shrimp or scallops to sauce, toss, and serve immediately.

Thai Curry Glaze

enough for 4 servings

➤ **NOTE:** *Look for Thai red curry paste near the rice noodles, coconut milk, and fish sauce in well-stocked grocery stores. Asian food stores will stock this item as well. Smash the lemon grass with the back of a chef's knife to release its flavor oils.*

1	teaspoon Thai red curry paste
½	cup coconut milk
2	medium garlic cloves, minced
2	teaspoons minced fresh gingerroot
1	piece lemon grass, 6-inches long, cut in half crosswise and bruised
2	teaspoons Asian fish sauce
2	teaspoons thinly sliced fresh basil leaves
	Salt and ground black pepper

In a small bowl, whisk curry paste into coconut milk; set aside. Follow Master Recipe for Sautéed Shrimp (page 86) or Scallops (page 88). Without discarding fat, set skillet over low heat. Add garlic, ginger, and lemon grass and sauté until fragrant, about 15 seconds. Increase heat to high and add curry-coconut milk mixture and fish sauce. Boil until liquid is reduced to 3 tablespoons, 3 to 4 minutes. Add any accumulated seafood juices and reduce sauce again to 3 tablespoons, cooking about 1 minute more. Remove lemon grass. Add basil and season with salt and pepper to taste. Add shrimp or scallops to sauce, toss, and serve immediately.

Spicy Nectarine Salsa
enough for 4 servings

2	medium nectarines, ripe but not mushy, cut into ¼-inch dice
¼	small red onion, minced (about 1 tablespoon)
½	medium jalapeño chile, stemmed, seeded, and minced (about 1 tablespoon)
2	teaspoons minced crystallized ginger
1	tablespoon golden raisins
1	tablespoon lime juice
2	tablespoons pineapple juice
	Salt

In a small bowl, combine all salsa ingredients, including salt to taste, until well blended. Allow to stand for 5 minutes to let flavors develop. Follow Master Recipe for Sautéed Shrimp (page 86) or Scallops (page 88). Spoon salsa over shrimp or scallops and serve immediately.

index